Belinda's Balloon

BELINDA'S BALLOON
A PICTURE CORGI 0 552 523542
First published in 1985 by William Heinemann Ltd.
Picture Corgi edition published 1986
Reprinted 1988 twice

Picture Corgi Books are published by Transworld Publishers Ltd.,
61-63 Uxbridge Road, Ealing, London W5 5SA
Printed and bound in Portugal by Printer Portuguesa

Belinda's Balloon

Emilie Boon

PICTURE CORGI BOOKS

One lovely summer's day the Bear family set off for a picnic in the park.

Father Bear and Lucy carried the picnic baskets. Mother Bear pushed Belinda in her pram.

They spread out the rug under some shady trees. Mother Bear made a daisychain for Lucy, while Father Bear bounced Belinda in the air.

Father and Mother Bear were tired and felt like having a nap.

"Can I take Belinda to buy a balloon?" asked Lucy.

"Yes, but do look after her," said Mother Bear.

So Lucy pushed the pram to the balloon-seller all by herself.

"I've got a special balloon just for you," said the balloon-seller, handing Belinda a big pink one.

Belinda held the string tight. But there was a sudden gust of wind and the balloon pulled the little bear up, up into the air.

"Come back!" cried Lucy.

But Belinda loved sailing through the air. She wasn't frightened at all.

Lucy tried to catch her, but the pink balloon drifted out of reach and into the treetops.

"What shall I do?" wailed Lucy as she ran after the balloon-seller. "Please help me to get my sister back!"

The balloon-seller gave her three big balloons.

"Don't be afraid," he said. "These balloons will help you find your sister."

"Oh, thank you," said Lucy.

Hanging on to the strings, she floated upwards. Where *was* Belinda?

She was soon in the treetops among the squirrels and birds. And there she saw Belinda, safe and sound, sitting on a branch, and munching a biscuit.

"Oh, Belinda, I've found you," said Lucy.
"Hullo, we're having a party," said a friendly squirrel. "Come and join us."
So Lucy sat down next to Belinda and they all had some tea.

"Well, we really must be going now," said Lucy when they had finished and could eat no more. "Thank you for a lovely party."

They waved goodbye to their friends and floated away.

Their tummies were so round and full that the balloons drifted downwards, and they landed gently on the soft grass.

"Mummy, Daddy, we're back!" shouted Lucy.

"Just in time for tea," said Mother Bear. "And what a beautiful balloon Belinda's got."

"It's a magic balloon," said Lucy. "It carried Belinda away, but I found her, and we had tea with a squirrel."

"I wonder if you've got room for another tea?" said Father Bear.

"Oh yes!" said Lucy.

So the little bears tucked into the picnic, and their tummies grew fuller and rounder than ever.

After tea Lucy helped put away the picnic things, and Belinda fell asleep. Then Lucy pushed the pram all the way home, and the magic balloon went with them.